THE FSEP

THE FAITH STANDARD & EVALUATION PROCESS

W. FRANK LARKINS JR.

THE FSEP

THE FAITH STANDARD & EVALUATION PROCESS

Inspired by an experience of humility – Honor!

This book was birthed from many humbling experiences in life. From childhood to adulthood, this book expresses my gratitude for God's grace and mercy on my life. For a wise man once said, and I paraphrase, "a man's reward is honor if he elects to live and accept a life of humility in God."

My hope for the reader is the discovery of God's unconditional love. As a son who was raised by a father, and now as a father raising children of my own, I can relate to a father's love. The characteristics of a father's love are unconditional, trustworthy, dependable, accountable, responsible, purposeful, merciful, and forgiving.

A father's greatest desire for a child is growth. The father loves his child through the development. The father's development process may consist of allowing the child to experience challenge, grief, loss, success, failure, etc. In addition to developing the child's decision making ability, self-esteem, resiliency, etc., the father is also strengthening the child's faith in him and his promise of unconditional love.

Likewise, this book takes the reader through the Father's process of faith development. The reader will gain a greater understanding and appreciation for life's challenges. Additionally, the reader will discover for the first time or be reminded of the Father's love for them.

Lastly, the reader will discover promises that will guarantee or confirm victory in past, present, and future challenges of humility onward to honor

God is the Commander of the 777th Battlefield Armory Wing. The Armory Wing is comprised of faithful laborers who specialize in treading out the paths for the next generation of believers to follow. These faithful laborers who are also known as Armor-Bearers are not to be muzzled. Additionally, they are worthy of their reward and honor from the Commander.[1]

This book is intended to challenge the reader's understanding of the things that may seem damning. For those who consider themselves to be laborers of God, then these setbacks are nothing more than a challenge of your faith. For those who understand the purpose of challenge, they know there is a reward on the backend of the challenge.

The Commander is the giver of all, the owner and inspiration of all things. Faith is the laborer's request to God for a blessing to be poured upon him or her. In return, God challenges the sincerity of faith to justify the continued pouring of blessings, which explains the reward that follows the challenge. God challenges those He loves to lead, inspire, and motivate laborers into action. What good is faith without an outward expression? Faith is dead without works.[2]

Lastly, the laborer must be knowledgeable of those God employs to validate and verify (VAL/VER) the faith of His laborers. God's most dependable agent in VAL/VER'ing the laborer's faith is Satan. Satan's "go-to" method of choice is fear. Fortunately enough for the laborer, the spirit of fear is not an attribute of the Commander and therefore, not of the laborer.

Successful challenges are guaranteed or your money back with a mustard-seed size of faith.

This book provides a gated process approach to the Commander's Faith Validation and Verification Process. The writer leads, inspires, and motivates the reader to see a challenge, accept the challenge as the Commander's way of validating and verifying the reader's faith. Additionally, the reader will be encouraged to persevere through Satan's orchestrated faith challenge(s) in confidence and assurance.

The Commander made many promises to the laborer that assures a successful outcome. The Commander's FSEP provides the reader with ten promises to ensure the integrity of his/her faith.

CONTENTS

CHAPTER ONE

ACCEPTING THE CHALLENGE

God is the Commander of the 777th Battlefield Armory Wing. The Armory Wing is comprised of faithful laborers who specialize in treading out the paths for the next generation of believers to follow. These faithful laborers who are also known as Armor-Bearers are worthy of their reward and honor.[3] They have freely chosen to follow, worship, and lay down their lives for the purpose of influencing, commissioning, and ultimately transforming men and women from doubter to believer and onward becoming a Battlefield Amor-Bearer for the Lord. The Commander responds by blessing them that follow and appointing them beneficiaries of the promises made to their forefathers. However, with these promises comes the validation and verification of our faith, loyalty, and our love for God, the Commander.

Therefore, the Commander mandates His Armor-Bearers to be tested in effort of validating and verifying their promotion and increase of responsibility and servant leadership. Additionally, the validation and the verification process serves as God's way of sifting out or exposing false believers from the ranks. For humility comes before honor.[4] The hope is that once a false believer or doubter has been exposed, he or she would then confront their issue head-on and choose to follow and receive the Commander's honor. Once an Armor-Bearer's faith has been validated and verified by the Commander, it is then that the Armor-Bearer has his or her being.

There is nothing more important to the Commander than His Armor-Bearer's confidence in their faith to speak life or death into any situation on the battlefield. This confidence of faith is even more of grave importance on the road to salvation which can be a blood bath for those with little faith. The road to salvation is the likeness of a camel going through the eye of a needle.[5] Without abounding faith, this road may easily be perceived as a false sense of impossibility. This kind of power, authority, and responsibility is only bestowed to those the Commander trusts; those who have been proven to be True Believers. To be a True Believer is to be loyal and obedient to God's Rules of Engagement (ROE) – The Word of God.

In return for obedience and/or compliance to the ROEs, the Commander rewards his Armor-Bearers with His unwavering protection, provision, and fulfillment of promise. So, how does the Commander separate True Believers from amongst those that have wavered in their faith and from those who no longer believe but are living the life of an Armor-Bearer? How does the Commander separate True Armor-Bearers from the freeloaders or the bandwagoners of this world? He employs Satan, his son.[6]

The Commander puts Satan on assignment. Satan is tasked to stage situations that challenges the faith of the Armor-Bearer. These faith challenges allows the Commander as well as the Armor Bearer the opportunity to assess his or her faith and trust in the Commander's ROEs. In other words, our faith in God is validated and verified which ultimately justifies our rightful place in the Commander's Armed Services. Satan is permitted to seek and attempt to kill, and destroy the faith of believers wherever he can find them.[7] In turn, Satan reports to the Lord the Armor-Bearers who are faithful and who have withstood his temptations (i.e., self-glorification, vengeance, greed, etc.). For those Armor-Bearers who are able to withstand Satan's temptations are also rewarded with more responsibility, promotion, and honor by way of their testimony. It is extremely important for the Armor-Bearer to have a testimony accompanied by their faith in the blood of the Lamb in order for other Armor-Bearers to overcome their battles.[8]

The Commander has no respect of person when it comes to appointing authority and honor on future leaders. The reason for this transparent approach to leadership on the battlefield is due to labor in battle being plentiful and having few laborers of integrity.

The Commander desires a leader He can trust, a leader with Core Values[9]:

1) Integrity - trusting in the Commander's promises in their darkest hour.

2) Service Before Self - willing to be a living sacrifice, placing their desires second to the Will of the Commander.

3) Excellence in Works - doing all things to the glory of God for it is by works that faith lives.

CHAPTER TWO

GETTING THROUGH THE GATES

The Commander's Validation and Verification Process according to Job's testimony:

GATE I - The Armor-Bearer's Armed Service Entitlements:

Upon joining the Armed Services of the Most High God, all of the brave men and women are blessed with riches, safety, and great influence. During the Commander's address to his Armor-Bearer, he foot-stomps the risk of growing complacent while resting in the comforts and safety of His gates.

Additionally, he stresses the need for readiness. The Commander encourages his Armor-Bearer to be prepared in season and out of season. Three disciplines the Commander insists on for spiritual readiness are: 1) Study to show thyself approved, 2) Pray without ceasing, and 3) Perfect and put on the whole armor ensemble in battle.[10]   Additionally, each Armor-Bearer is provided a personalized copy of their orders, which is the Great Commission.

GATE II - Quality Control of the Believer:

The Commander appoints and employs Satan, the Officer in Charge (OIC) of the Faith Resiliency Department. Satan is dispatched to aide in VAL/VER'ing the faith of the Armor-Bearer in order for the Commander to justify the Armor-Bearer's entitlements. Satan's 'Go-To' method for attacking the faith of the Armor-Bearer is FEAR! Satan knows fear is the opposite of LOVE.

A fearful Armor-Bearer afraid of death in battle is likely to surrender and throw in the towel at first sight. Satan knows he can inflict the kind of fear and doubt in an Armor-Bearer's mind that would invoke a compromise of the Armor-Bearer's core values. Ultimately, fear would eventually overtake the Armor-Bearer's faith pushing them outside of the comforting gates of the Commander.

To be driven outside of the gates of the Commander is sin. It is worth noting that the death expectancy of the Armor-Bearer once they are outside of the gates of the Commander is like a vapor. The wages of sin is death.[11] Additionally, for those who have taken a sworn oath to defend the Constitution – the Gospel, and to subject themselves as a living sacrifice to the Commander are held strictly accountable for the bloodshed of their brothers in arm.[12]

GATE III - The Armor-Bearer's Faith Evaluation:

The Commander chooses the intensity level and category of faith evaluation according to the Armor-Bearer's current level of faith and purpose in battle. The Commander sees all and knows all and selects who He chooses to promote, demote, and/or reassign in battle for His glory which ultimately serves current and future Armor-Bearers for generations to come. Nonetheless, the Commander's decisions are based on the faith of the Armor-Bearer. It is by faith the Armor-Bearer is justified and sanctified by the Commander.[13]

Upon request of the evaluation, Satan performs a profile review of the individual chosen by God. What Satan is looking for are areas of opportunity easily to persuade the Armor-Bearer into denouncing the Commander.

The profile review may consist of but is not limited to: 1) recalling the Armor-Bearer's history of loyalty or trust in the Commander, 2) whether or not the Armor-Bearer is within the Commander's gates of protection, and 3) the Armor-Bearer's skill level or ability to use their armor in defense of their faith.

These areas of interest are key to successfully coming out of Satan's test of faith stronger and wiser than before. Satan knows that the Armor-Bearer increases their chances of successfully passing the test if they have not fallen victim to complacency but instead have been diligent in studying to show themselves approved - craftsman in armorship.

GATE IV - Inspector's Recommendation:

Satan, the Faith Resiliency Officer, provides a recommendation and assessment of the Armor-Bearer to the Commander. Satan is also known to be the most cunning Armor-Bearer of them all. Hence why Satan is extremely confident in his ability to seek, kill, and destroy the faith of a believer by fearing them into submission. Therefore, Satan boasts of his ability in deceiving the most loyal Armor-Bearers into discrediting the Commander.

But, the Commander also has confidence. The Commander's confidence rests in the bloodshed and the testimony of His Only Begotten Son, Jesus.[14] The Commander knows that the Armor-Bearers shall overcome if they hold to their faith and to every word of their testimony. Knowing every Armor-Bearer has heard the gospel of Jesus and how Jesus's faith also matched his works. Jesus, being the most feared Armor-Bearer of them all, never compromised his faith to death.

The Commander is confident that the servant leadership in Jesus will inspire his Armor-Bearers to persevere through any faith assessment of Satan. Additionally, the Commander's confidence rests in the testimonies of other pioneers that have treaded out the grain for the Armor-Bearer of today.

The Commander desires for each and every one of His Armor-Bearers to live and not die. The Commander recalls reminding every Armor-Bearer on the day they were sworn in, that they will surely overcome any challenge if only they receive the Blood of the Lamb and the testimonies of their forefathers. This confirmation of faith is only another act of reassurance for the Commander.

Lastly, the Commander knows that the evaluation is only a measuring tool of faith and His way of developing those that love Him for great things in life. The one sure thing the Commander knows that the Armor-Bearer may or may not know but certainly doesn't' believe is, Satan does not have jurisdiction over the body. Satan is only a tester of faith and does not have the power to physically kill the body of an Armor-Bearer unless the Armor-Bearer relinquishes this power unto Satan.

The Commander is a keeper of his promises. Therefore, even after the relinquishment of power unto Satan, the Armor-Bearer is still entitled to the promise if he or she chooses to return to the ranks of the Commander. Henceforth, the Commander educated his Armor-Bearers on the principles of humility, honor, and pride. The Commander ensured that all Armor-Bearers understood the proverb, "Humility comes before Honor and Pride comes before the Fall."[15] Additionally, the Commander seizes moments in each Armor-Bearer's life on a daily basis to reassure his promise to never leave nor forsake them who willfully choose to love Him and obey His commandments.[16]

GATE V - Personnel Performance:

The 10 Rules of Engagement (ROEs) ordered by the Commander whenever a Armor-Bearer find themselves in the valley of the shadow of death or temptation are to: 1) Hold fast to God's unchanging hand, 2) Remain faithful to the promises of God, 3) Remember the joy of the Lord on the day you swore to fight the good fight of faith, 4) Know that you have been chosen for greater works and a higher calling, 5) Trust the report of the Lord, 6) Not be afraid for the spirit of fear is not of God, 7) Fight for the testimony of the only Begotten Son, 8) Perpetuate faith by resisting Satan's obstacles, 9) Love those that curse and persecute you, and 10) Love your neighbor as yourself – FIGHT FOR FAITH!

GATE VI - The Commander's Response:

God is the Commander. The Commander is the Judge. The Commander determines the fate of those that serve him. The Commander also recognizes those who willfully choose to rely on their faith and perform in ways that brings credit upon themselves, their beloved (i.e., family, friends, organization, etc.), the Armed Services, and the Commander.

The Commander has a way of making up for inconveniencing or humiliating his Armor-Bearers on the battlefield. He honors those who he chastises in the presence of their enemies (Psalm 23:5). Additionally, the Commander appoints the successful Armor-Bearer to a higher calling of servant leadership. He restores the Armor-Bearer with all that was lost plus a bonus. Furthermore, the Commander recognizes and blesses those that supported, encouraged, and prayed for the Armor-Bearer during their faith challenge. Lastly, the Commander encourages the Armor-Bearer to continue studying to show themselves approved for even higher levels of responsibility and leadership. To whom much is given, much is required.[17]

GATE VII – The Armor-Bearer's Response:

The Armor-Bearer's response after an encounter with Satan ordered by the Commander is to: 1) Remain faithful, 2) Remain humble, 3) Remain in love with his or her Commander, 4) Be proud of his or her accomplishments, 5) Present yourself as a living sacrifice to the Commander and to them you lead in battle, and 6) Serve those who desire to serve alongside of you in battle.

The life of the Armor-Bearer following a successful encounter with Satan is that of a living testimony. The discipleship of men by way of the testimony is the Commander's return on investment.[18] Lastly, the Armor-Bearer is further encouraged to maintain a level of spiritual readiness by studying to show themselves approved.[19]

In order to successfully maintain spiritual readiness, the Armor-Bearer should periodically conduct a self-assessment and command a transformation of the areas where their proverbial walls of faith have been compromised. The Armor-Bearer must always remember God's grace which is freely given to all men.

The Commander so loved the world that he graced his only begotten Son, Jesus, into battle to die the death that was intended for all men due to their lack of faith. By gracing Jesus into battle, the Commander knew the future Armor-Bearer would be granted a new entitlement and promise – "everlasting life."

With this entitlement and promise, the Commander's return on investment will be secured, the soul of every Armor-Bearer will be returned to the Commander and the Armor-Bearer will be given a proper place in the Commander's quarters. However, like any other entitlement or promise given of the Commander, it is received by choice and not by force. In other words, the Commander freely offers in love and men freely choose to receive by faith. Since the Commander is the owner of all entitlements and resources freely given to the Armor-

Bearer, he is obligated to himself to monitor and justify the acquisition of heavenly resources. The Commander calls all men to follow him. "If anyone would come after me, let him deny himself and take up his cross and follow me. For whoever would save his life for my sake will find it."[20]

CHAPTER THREE

PERSONNEL EVALUATION

In case you find yourself before the Commander's promotion board, handpicked for an evaluation of your faith, cling to God's promises. Additionally, do not be afraid. For God did not design you to carry the spiritual gene of fear. Instead, you were outfitted to perfection in His likeness; designed for power, love, and of a sound mind.[21]

Here are ten promises or entitlements for those whose faith allows them to believe:

1. Promise for Resiliency:

"Be strong and of a good courage, fear not, nor be afraid of them: for the Lord thy God, he it is that doth go with thee; he will not fail thee, nor forsake thee."[22]

2. Promise for Shelter

"All that the Father giveth me shall come to me; and him that cometh to me I will in no wise cast out."[23]

Promise for Relationship

"For I am persuaded, that neither death, nor life, nor angels nor principalities, nor powers, no things present, nor things to come, nor height, nor depth, nor any other creature, shall be able to separate us from the love of God, which is in Christ Jesus our Lord."[24]

3. Promise for Forgiveness

"If we confess our sins, he is faithful and just to forgive us our sins, and to cleanse us from all unrighteousness."[25]

4. Promise for Mercy

"For he hath made him to be sin for us, who knew no sin; that we might be made the righteousness of God in him."[26]

5. Promise for Prosperity

"And we know that all things work together for good to them that love God, to them who are the called according to his purpose."[27]

6. Promise for Grace

"But God commendeth his love toward us, in that, while we were yet sinners, Christ died for us."[28]

7. Promise for Honor

"Humble yourselves therefore under the mighty hand of God, that he may exalt you in due time: Casting all your care upon him; for he careth for you."[29]

8. Promise for Bravery

"Fear thou not; for I am with thee: be not dismayed; for I am thy God; I will strengthen thee; yea, I will help thee yea, I will uphold thee with the right hand of my righteousness."[30]

9. Promise for Faith

"Jesus said unto her, I am the resurrection, and the life: he that believeth in me, though he were dead, yet shall he live: And whosoever liveth and believeth in me shall never die. Believest thou this."[31]

____

CHAPTER FOUR

THE SITUATIONAL REPORT

My wife, the mother of my children, the why of my drive, and the gem of the space she occupies was diagnosed with cancer – carcinoid tumors. At that moment, I knew the Commander had chosen us, the Larkins' Family, to undergo an FSEP. Individually and collectively, we were in contention with the greatest tester of faith, Satan.

After years of being battlefield tested, LaShanna and I had decided to live a life of accountability to ourselves and to those we encounter. Additionally, we made a pact which became our family motto and then transformed it into what is now our Life Management Consulting strategy, to be Purposeful, Timely, and Legendary in all things. Our hope as individuals, a couple, and a family is to influence, inspire, and inject an awakening of God into the lives of those we come in contact with.

Our conviction was simple, the pursuit of purpose. We leaned on the scriptures and not our own understanding.[32] We found ourselves having the desire to make a difference with the life we have remaining. Understanding that God equates our life expectancy to that of a vapor.[33] We agreed to commit to purpose, stewardship of time, and be deliberate about the legacy or impact we gift to those we love. Therefore, we challenged ourselves to be timely, giving no care for tomorrow but instead making a difference on today.[34] We have clung to these disciplines in honor of our Commander, God the Father.

The Larkins' family has been actively spreading the Gospel; influencing, inspiring, and injecting the spirit of God abroad and throughout communities, homes, and the local schools and churches. During this particular time, I, Capt Larkins, was deployed with the U.S. Air Force to an undisclosed location in Southwest Asia. While deployed, I devoted time towards leading bible studies, teaching marriage and family disciplines, and leading worship services all while being a servant leader on the job.

LaShanna, well, she was the epitome of a virtuous woman. She worked a full-time job, singlehandedly raising, feeding, protecting, and instructing our two children, Lauren and Logan. Additionally, LaShanna ensured the kids ate balanced meals, attended the various after-school activities, and maintained a healthy spiritual experience. LaShanna and the kids sustained a healthy lifestyle in my absence which in-turn honored God and His promise to never leave her nor forsake her in a time of need.[35]

Then it happened, the Commander directed FSEP. The FSEP was to be conducted on the Larkins' family. Before God could increase our territory of responsibility, the faith that we exuded had to be VAL/VER'd. What better time to evaluate our faith then now when our family was separated and most vulnerable. Satan was confident in his ability to fear us into submission. He was destined to discredit our faith, ultimately stealing, killing, and destroying the faith of those who had decided to follow God as a result of witnessing our works of faith.

On December 14, 2017 while deployed, I was called out of my morning meeting to take an important phone call. "Hello", I answered. The voice on the opposite end of the phone was my Commander. He replied, "Please remain calm. LaShanna is in the hospital and the kids are with friends." Immediately, I went from zero to sixty. "Say what!" I replied. "What happened?" My first response was to panic. I began to feel the weight of guilt coming over me. I was being deceived into feeling guilty for not being with LaShanna as her protector. Instead, I prayed with my Commanding

Officer and began to pull strength from our faith. In prayer, I was reminded of God being our protector and comforter.[36] At that very moment, I knew that the time had come for our family to activate our faith for our FSEP. I was relieved of my deployment and redeployed to be with my family during this time.

Upon my return, LaShanna was still in the hospital. The day prior, she had emergency surgery due to abdominal obstruction. One week after the procedure, the biopsy results were released. The doctor broke the news to LaShanna. The biopsy confirmed traces of carcinoid tumors. She was ordered to consult with an Oncologist.

This was the kind of news that would induce fear for the faithless. Fear is Satan's weapon of choice. Unfortunately for him, fear is not a weapon that can infiltrate skilled Armor-Bearers, those who have been battle tested. We remained faithful. Even after the Oncologist validated and verified the doctor's report, we remained faithful. LaShanna was scheduled to see the Oncologist the following month to determine tumor activity and potential treatment. This was Satan's way of putting us in the refiner's fire. We had to live with knowing LaShanna's body was infected with cancer for thirty days before receiving the Oncologist's report – the test.

Satan then sucker punched us while we were already down. Because we refused to curse God, we were tried again. But, this time my entire family was directly impacted. We had a house fire.

On January 16, 2018, we had a house fire that damaged approximately forty percent of our home. There was no physical harm to our family. Although another tragedy for the Larkins' family, I saw it as another opportunity to prove God's promises are true.   Having experienced now two very significant life altering tragedies, we began to discern doubt in the words of some of our closest friends and loved ones. It was at that moment we knew we needed to pass this FSEP for their faith just as much as for our own. We were secure in our faith and in the promises of God. Therefore, we knew it was only a test of our faith after boldly proclaiming God publicly and shamelessly. Also, we believed we were being chosen by God for greater works, hence why He was testing our faith.

Now, the time had come for LaShanna's follow-up appointment and scan interpretation. This was the time when a man with lukewarm faith would have been challenged the most. Despite our outward praise and confidence in knowing God would not forsake us, we still discerned doubters of God's promises. Their faith would be described as being lukewarm.[37] Knowing this, LaShanna and I pulled closer and we turned our prayers towards our friends and loved ones. We went into our appointment, our proverbial Lion's Den, believing and came out without a scratch. LaShanna's body did not have a single trace of cancer. The Oncologist released her the same day with high confidence that the surgical extraction removed the tumors.

LaShanna's faith fulfilled her healing. Her healing increased the faith of the doubters. The increased faith of the doubters glorified God. The glory unto God VAL/VER'd our faith and justified God's decision to increase our territory on His battlefield.

The Commander restored our family with an Armor-Bearer's share of entitlements. Additionally, we were blessed with an incredible U.S. Air Force special duty assignment, Education With Industry (EWI), after being told it wouldn't happen. Additionally, our home is being remodeled with the luxuries we desire to have in our home. And most importantly, our spiritual growth and newfound relationships with our community and believers have grown exponentially. As we, the Larkins' Family, look back over our life, we can see how God continues to use tragedies and challenges in our lives as launching pads to answering our prayers. Because of it, we have successfully passed another FSEP.

1 "For the scripture saith, Thou shalt not muzzle the ox that treadeth out the corn. And, The labourer is worthy of his reward"…1 Timothy 5:18. The Holy Bible. King James Version

2 "Even so faith, if it hath not works, is dead, being alone"…James 2:17. The Holy Bible. King James Version

3 "For the scripture saith, Thou shalt not muzzle the ox that treadeth out the corn. And, The labourer is worthy of his reward"…1 Timothy 5:18. The Holy Bible. King James Version

4 "The fear of the Lord is the instruction of wisdom; and before honour is humility"…Proverbs 15:33. The Holy Bible. King James Version

5 "And again I say unto you, It is easier for a camel to go through the eye of a needle, than for a rich man to enter into the kingdom of God"…Matthew 19:24. The Holy Bible. King James Version

6 "Now there was a day when the sons of God came to present themselves before the Lord, and Satan came also among them"…Job 1:6. The Holy Bible. King James Version

7 "The thief cometh not, but for to steal, and to kill, and to destroy: I am come that they might have life, and that they might have it more abundantly"…John 10:10. The Holy Bible. King James Version

8 "And they overcame him by the blood of the Lamb, and by the word of their testimony; and they loved not their lives unto the death"…Revelations 12:11. The Holy Bible. King James Version

9 "The Air Force Core Values are Integrity First, Service Before Self, and Excellence In All We Do"…Air Force Standards. Air Force Instruction 1-1.

10 "(10) Finally, my brethren, be strong in the Lord, and in the power of his might. (11) Put on the whole armour of God, that ye may be able to stand against the wiles of the devil. (12) For we wrestle not against flesh and blood, but against principalities, against powers, against spiritual wickedness in high places. (13) Wherefore take unto you the whole armour of God, that ye may be able to withstand in the evil day, and having done all, to stand. (14) Stand therefore, having your loins girt about with truth, and having on the breastplate of righteousness; (15) And your feet shod with the preparation of the gospel of peace; (16) Above all, taking the shield of faith, wherewith ye shall be able to quench all the fiery darts of the wicked. (17) And take the helmet of salvation, and the sword of the Spirit, which is the word of God: (18) Praying always with all prayer and supplication in the Spirit, and watching thereunto with all perseverance and supplication for all saints"…Ephesians 6: 10-18. The Holy Bible. King James Version

11 "For the wages of sin is death; but the gift of God is eternal life through Jesus Christ our Lord"…Romans 6:23. The Holy Bible. King James Version

12 "Brethren, if a man be overtaken in a fault, ye which are spiritual, restore such an one in the spirit of meekness;

considering thyself, lest thou also be tempted"…Galatians 6:1. The Holy Bible. King James Version

13 "Therefore being justified by faith, we have peace with God through our Lord Jesus Christ"…Romans 5:1. The Holy Bible. King James Version

14 "For God so loved the world, that he gave his only begotten Son, that whosoever believeth in him should not perish, but have everlasting life"…John 3:16. The Holy Bible. King James Version

15 "Before destruction the heart of man is haughty, and before honour is humility"…Proverbs 18:12. The Holy Bible. King James Version

16 "And Samuel said, Hath the Lord as great delight in burnt offerings and sacrifices, as in obeying the voice of the Lord? Behold, to obey is better than sacrifice, and to hearken than the fat of rams"…I Samuel 15:22. The Holy Bible. King James Version

17 "But he that knew not, and commit things worthy of stripes, shall be beaten with few stripes. For unto whomsoever much is given, of him shall be much required: and to whom men have committed much, of him they will ask the more"…Luke 12:48. The Holy Bible. King James Version

18 "And he saith unto them, Follow me, and I will make you fishers of men"…Matthew 4:19. The Holy Bible. King James Version

19 "Study to show thyself approved unto God, a workman that needeth not to be ashamed, rightly dividing the word of truth"…II Timothy 2:15. The Holy Bible. King James Version

20 "(24) Then said Jesus unto his disciples, If any man will come after me, let him deny himself, and take up his cross, and follow me. (25) For whosoever will save his life shall lose it: and whosoever will lose his life for my sake shall find it"…Matthew 16:24-25. The Holy Bible. King James Version

21 "For God hath not given us the spirit of fear; but of power, and of love, and of a sound mind"…II Timothy 1:7. The Holy Bible. Authorized King James Version

22 "Be strong and of a good courage, fear not, nor be afraid of them: for the Lord thy God, he it is that doth go with thee; he will not fail thee, nor forsake thee"…Deuteronomy 31:6. The Holy Bible. Authorized King James Version

23 "All that the Father giveth me shall come to me; and him that cometh to me I will in no wise cast out"…John 6:37. The Holy Bible. Authorized King James Version

24 "(38) For I am persuaded, that neither death, nor life, nor angles nor principalities, nor powers, no things present, nor things to come, (39) nor height, nor depth, nor any other creature, shall be able to separate us from the love of God, which is in Christ Jesus our Lord"…Romans 8:38-39. The Holy Bible. Authorized King James Version

25 "If we confess our sins, he is faithful and just to forgive us our sins, and to cleanse us from all unrighteousness"…1 John 1:9. The Holy Bible. Authorized King James Version

26 "For he hath made him to be sin for us, who knew no sin; that we might be made the righteousness of God in him"…II Corinthians 5:21. The Holy Bible. Authorized King James Version

27 "And we know that all things work together for good to them that love God, to them who are the called according to his purpose"…Romans 8:28. The Holy Bible. Authorized King James Version

28 "But God commendeth his love toward us, in that, while we were yet sinners, Christ died for us"…Romans 5:8. The Holy Bible. Authorized King James Version

29 "(6) Humble yourselves therefore under the mighty hand of God, that he may exalt you in due time: (7) Casting all your care upon him; for he careth for you"…I Peter 5:6-7. The Holy Bible. Authorized King James Version

30 "Fear thou not; for I am with thee: be not dismayed; for I am thy God; I will strengthen thee; yea, I will help thee yea, I will uphold thee with the right hand of my righteousness"…Isaiah 41:10. The Holy Bible. Authorized King James Version

31 "(25) Jesus said unto her, I am the resurrection, and the life: he that believeth in me, though he were dead, yet shall he live: (26) And whosoever liveth and believeth in me shall never die. Believest thou this"…John 11:25-26. The Holy Bible. Authorized King James Version

32 "Trust in the Lord with all thine heart; and lean not unto thine own understanding"…Proverbs 3:5. The Holy Bible. King James Version 33 "Whereas ye know not what shall be on the morrow, For what is your life? It is even a vapour, that appeareth for a little time, and then vanisheth away"…James 4:14. The Holy Bible. King James Version

34 "Take therefore no thought for the morrow: for the morrow shall take thought for the things of itself. Sufficient unto the day is the evil thereof"…Matthew 6:34. The Holy Bible. King James Version

35 "Be strong and of a good courage, fear not, nor be afraid of them: for the Lord thy God, he it is that doth go with thee; he will not fail thee, nor forsake thee"…Deuteronomy 31:6. The Holy Bible. King James Version

36 "The Lord is my rock, and my fortress, and my deliverer; my God, my strength, in whom I will trust; my buckler, and the horn of my salvation, and my high tower"…Psalm 18:2. The Holy Bible. King James Version

37 "So then because thou art lukewarm, and neither cold nor hot, I will spew thee out of my mouth"…Revelation 3:16. The Holy Bible. King James Version